CREATURES OF THE PAST

CREATURES OF THE PAST

Written by
CECILIA FITZSIMONS

Illustrated by
CHRIS FORSEY

RSVP
RAINTREE
STECK-VAUGHN
PUBLISHERS
The Steck-Vaughn Company

Austin, Texas

Published by Raintree Steck-Vaughn, an imprint of Steck-Vaughn Company

Library of Congress Cataloging-in-Publication Data

Fitzsimons, Cecilia

Creatures of the past / written by Cecilia Fitzsimons; illustrated by Chris Forsey

p. cm. — (Nature's hidden worlds)

Includes index.

Summary: Text and picture puzzles provide information about many different prehistoric creatures, including early fishes, amphibians, reptiles, dinosaurs, and mammals.

ISBN 0-8172-3970-7 (Hardcover)

ISBN 0-8172-4184-1 (Softcover)

1. Animals, Fossil—Juvenile literature.

[1. Prehistoric animals. 2. Picture puzzles.] I. Forsey, Christopher, ill. II. Title. III. Series.

QE765.F57 1996   95-444

566—dc20   CIP AC

Note to reader

There are some words in this book that are printed in **bold** type. You will find the meanings for each of these words in the glossary on page 46.

Designer: Mike Jolley

Project Editor: Wendy Madgwick

Editor: Kim Merlino

Printed in Italy

1 2 3 4 5 6 7 8 9 LB 99 98 97 96

Introduction

This book illustrates the prehistoric world. Each picture involves a puzzle. Swim in the Devonian seas, about 400 million years ago. Or join Tyrannosaurus in a fight. Spot the differences between two pictures of the same scene. Match up the creature with its food or footprints. Did those animals really live then? Solve the puzzles and find out about creatures of the past.

Contents

Cenozoic Era

Quaternary Period
2 million-present years ago
Tertiary Period
65-2 million years ago

Mesozoic Era

Cretaceous Period
144-65 million years ago

Jurassic Period
213-144 million years ago

Triassic Period
248-213 million years ago

Permian Period
286-248 million years ago

Carboniferous Period
360-286 million years ago

Paleozoic Era

Devonian Period
408-360 million years ago

Silurian Period
438-408 million years ago

Ordovician Period
505-438 million years ago

Cambrian Period
590-505 million years ago

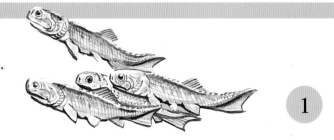

Age of Fish

Four hundred million years ago the best developed animals were fish. At that time, fish were the some of the largest creatures in the world. Look carefully at the pictures below of water life in Devonian times. Can you spot ten differences between the scenes?

The earliest fish did not have biting and chewing jaws. Their mouths were like suckers. Many of them had no fins and their **skeleton** was made of **cartilage**, not bone. Their heads and often their bodies were protected by hard bony plates. The many kinds of jawless fish mostly ate tiny plants. Some of the fish were hunted by animals such as huge sea scorpions and squidlike Orthoceras.

Fish with jaws and teeth appeared about 80 million years after these jawless fish first lived. By Devonian times, the Age of Fish some 400 million years ago, many kinds of fish were plentiful. Some were fierce hunters. Others were their **prey**.

Ancient Waters

Did you spot the differences?

1 The teeth of Dunkleosteus are different.

2 Bothriolepis's limb has moved.

3 Cephalaspis is sucking up a stream of mud.

4 Pteraspis now has a smaller spine on its back.

5 Cladoselache's mouth is now open.

6 Another Moythomasia fish is present.

7 Dipnorhynchus now has bubbles of air.

8 Eusthenopteron's tail now has two prongs not three.

9 Coelacanthus has a fin missing.

10 An Orthoceras is swimming in the water.

Living fossil

Scientists were very surprised when a living coelacanth, named Latimeria, was caught near Madagascar in 1938. These fish live in very deep water near the island. Hundreds of coelacanths have been caught and a few have been filmed. But we still know very little about how these fish live.

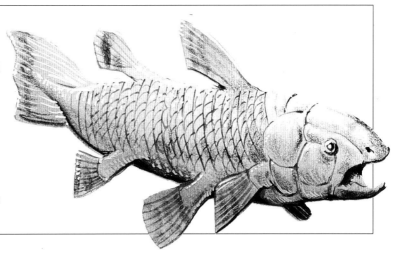

Some Devonian fish probably lived in fresh water. Pteraspis had a large head shield but no paired fins. It was a strong swimmer and fed in surface waters. Cephalaspis may have lived on the river bed and sucked up mud. Both fish had three "eyes"! The third "eye," a patch on top of the head, could possibly sense light.

Bothriolepis may also have lived on the riverbed. Its shoulders and head were covered with bony plates. The front fins were like a pair of spines. The fish may have used them like stilts to crawl over the mud.

Many other fish lived in the oceans. Cladoselache was similar to today's shark, but its fins and tail were different. Like the shark, its skeleton was made of cartilage not bone. The "Jaws" of the Devonian

oceans was Dunkleosteus and its relatives. These monsters grew up to 20 feet (6 m) long. Dunkleosteus could open its huge mouth very wide. It could also rock its head back to open its jaws even wider.

Moythomasia was an early bony fish. Its body scales could move against each other. They formed a flexible coat of armor.

Many fish, such as Coelacanthus, had lobed fins. Their paired, fleshy fins had large bones surrounded by muscles. Eusthenopteron may have been like the **ancestor** of land-living amphibians. The front and rear fins were almost like simple legs.

Dipnorhynchus, an early lung fish, had simple lungs like a land animal. It breathed air if the water became stagnant or shallow.

Age of Amphibians

Amphibians were the first large animals to crawl onto land. They first did so about 360 million years ago. Look carefully at the picture opposite. Can you find ten animals or plants that did not live in their swampy forest home?

The first plants took root on land about 460 million years ago. By Carboniferous times, about 360–286 million years ago, there were many land plants. These slowly developed into a great many different types of plants.

By the Age of Amphibians, swampy rain forests grew over land that now forms much of Europe and North America. The trees that grew there were simple plants, such as ferns, tree ferns, and fossil trees that no longer live.

Flowering plants did not appear until about 200 million years later. Flowering water plants appeared even later when some "land" plants in wet areas slowly became **adapted** to life in fresh water.

The first four-legged animal?

Fossils of an animal called Acanthostega were found in 1952. They are the earliest remains ever found of a four-legged animal. This 39-inch (1-m) long creature had fishlike gills and a tail with a fin. It probably spent most of its life in water. It may have had lungs too, for taking in air when it crawled onto land. These fossils have shown scientists that feet first developed in animals that lived in water rather than animals that lived on land.

On to Land

Ichthyostega (A) was one of the first amphibians. It still had the tail fin and bony scales of its fishlike ancestors. It lived on land and in water. Long-tailed Keraterpeton (B) and Eogyrinus (C) lived mainly in the water. Eogyrinus looked like a large salamander. It grew to 15 feet (4.5 m) and lived mostly in water. It may have hunted like a crocodile.

Pholidogaster (D) and Eryops (E) lived more on land. Eryops walked with its limbs held at right angles. Its heavy head would have been hard to lift up off the ground. So Eryops probably fed in the water.

What's wrong?

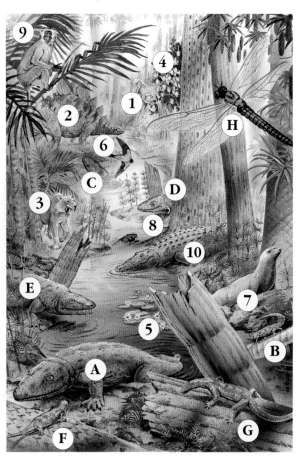

Dinosaurs, birds, mammals, and flowering plants had not yet appeared on Earth:

1 Tyrannosaurus rex lived in the Cretaceous Period, about 150 million years later.
2 Stegosaurus also lived in the Cretaceous.
3 The saber-toothed tiger lived in the Pleistocene, about 2 million years ago. No mammals lived in the Carboniferous.
4 The magnolia, one of the first flowering plants, did not appear until the Cretaceous.
5 A water lily is a modern flowering, freshwater plant.
6 The swallow, a modern bird, catches insects over water.
7 A modern seal lives in oceans.
8 A modern coypu lives in rivers.
9 A spider monkey from the rain forest of South America.
10 A Nile crocodile from Africa.

Amphibians lay their eggs in water. The eggs hatch into tadpoles (**larvae**) that can only live in water. Their feathery gills cannot work in the air. Branchiosaurus (F) may have been a tadpole. Fossils of this small creature show that it also had feathery gills. Amphibians had to return to water to breed, so they could not stray far from fresh water.

Most reptiles lay eggs on land. They were the first large animals that could live all their lives out of water. Hylonomus (G) was an early reptile that lived in Carboniferous swamps.

Flightless insects first appeared during Devonian times. They quickly spread across the land. By Carboniferous times many winged insects had developed. Meganeura (H) was an enormous dragonfly that flew through the swampy forest. Its wingspan was up to 28 inches (70 cm) across.

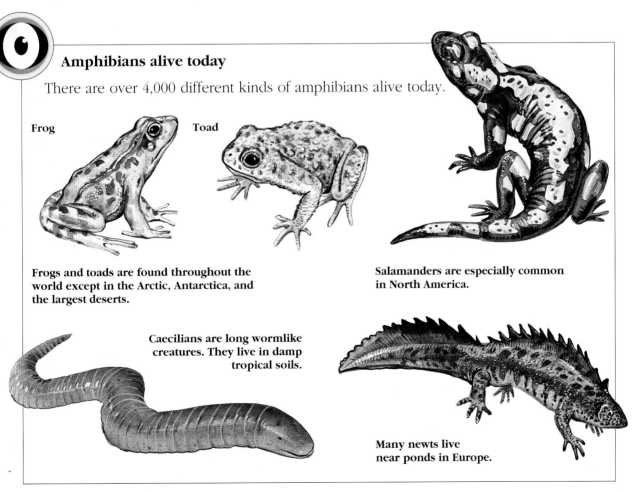

Amphibians alive today

There are over 4,000 different kinds of amphibians alive today.

Frog

Toad

Frogs and toads are found throughout the world except in the Arctic, Antarctica, and the largest deserts.

Salamanders are especially common in North America.

Caecilians are long wormlike creatures. They live in damp tropical soils.

Many newts live near ponds in Europe.

Reptiles Rule

During the Triassic Period, reptiles began to take over the land. Most reptiles lay their eggs on land. Look at the picture opposite. Can you match the five reptiles in the small pictures with their trails? Which animal does the nest belong to?

During the Triassic Period, about 225 million years ago, reptiles spread across the land. Reptile eggs have a tough leathery shell. This keeps the liquid inside the egg from drying out. It means that reptiles do not have to return to water to breed. They can lay their eggs on dry land. Reptiles were able to make their homes in both wet and dry land **habitats**.

Chasmatosaurus lived on the shores of rivers and lakes. It may have looked and swum like a modern crocodile. Its jaws were lined with sharp backward-pointing teeth. These teeth were ideal for catching fish. Chasmatosaurus walked like a lizard. Its four short legs spread out to the side of its body. It probably laid its eggs on land.

The race to rule

During the Triassic Period, the largest animals belonged to the group called mammal-like reptiles. The ancestors of the dinosaurs were still only small. When the mammal-like reptiles died out, why did dinosaurs and not the shrew-like mammals take over as the ruling animals? No one is sure, but it was probably because the climate became hotter and drier. Dinosaurs were possibly better suited to live in these conditions.

Lagosuchus, a reptile, may have been like the ancestor of dinosaurs.

Troodon, a dinosaur

Land Lubbers

Euparkia was a small meat-eating reptile. It usually walked on all four legs. When danger threatened, Euparkeria may have stood upright on its back legs to run away. It probably held its long tail stretched out behind to balance it. This small **predator** had sharp teeth to tear at the meat of its prey.

Did you follow the footprints?

1 Chasmatosaurus; the nest belonged to this reptile.
2 Euparkia.
3 Cynognathus.
4 Kannemeyeria.
5 Lagosuchus.

Lagosuchus was a slim animal with long legs. It was only about the size of a chicken. Its back legs were longer than the front ones. This suggests that Lagosuchus stood upright on two legs when it ran from danger. Some scientists believe it may have been the ancestor of the dinosaurs.

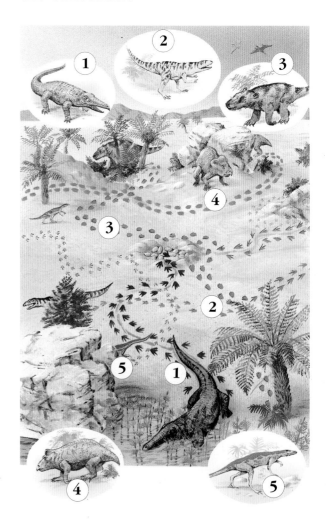

Small beginnings

During the Permian and Triassic Periods the mammal-like reptiles were the most successful group of animals on land. By the end of the Triassic, many of these reptiles had died out. They began to be replaced by the dinosaurs.

Mammals are warm-blooded, furry animals whose young suckle milk. The first mammals were tiny shrewlike creatures that developed from the mammal-like reptiles. These early mammals ate insects and lived in the undergrowth, hiding under logs and rocks or up trees. After the dinosaurs died out, these tiny creatures took over. They gradually gave rise to all the later mammals.

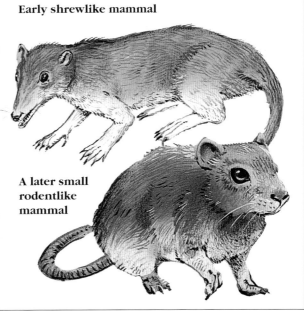

Early shrewlike mammal

A later small rodentlike mammal

Another large group of Triassic reptiles were called the mammal-like reptiles. The ancestors of the mammals probably arose from this group. Kannemeyeria was a large grazing animal about the size of an ox. It may have used its powerful horny beak to tear up leaves and roots. Then it ground up the plants by the shearing action of its toothless jaws. These reptiles probably lived in a herd like buffalo do today.

Cynognathus was a fierce meat-eater. It may have looked like a huge wolf with very powerful jaws and sharp teeth. Its head was over a foot long! Like a modern dog, its teeth were of different sizes and types. Sharp teeth at the front may have been used for stabbing and cutting. The flatter back teeth were used for chewing. It is also possible that Cynognathus had fur like mammals.

Many experts think that an animal related to Cynognathus was the ancestor of the true mammals. Reptiles are **cold-blooded** animals. They warm up and cool down as the weather around them gets hotter and colder. We do not know whether the mammal-like reptiles were cold-blooded or **warm-blooded** like us. Some scientists think that they were warm-blooded.

Rulers
of the Seas

Many large reptiles returned to the ocean and made it their home. Look at this picture of the ocean in Late Jurassic times. Can you spot the eight animals or objects that should not be there?

Today few reptiles live in the oceans. Only **marine** turtles, sea snakes, and one species of lizard, the marine iguana, live there. In Jurassic and Cretaceous times, the oceans were home to several kinds of sea reptiles. Many were well adapted to living in water. Their bodies were long and **streamlined**. Instead of legs, they had large flexible flippers. They probably used these to "fly" through the water like penguins do today.

Many of these reptiles were large and spent most of their life at sea. Some probably still laid their eggs on land. They may have moved like a modern sea lion. Like turtles today, they probably laid their eggs in holes on sandy beaches.

Beneath the Waves

Did you find all eight animals or objects?

1 A sea lion is a modern marine mammal.
2 A penguin is a modern bird.
3 A killer whale is a modern marine mammal.
4 A dolphin is a modern water mammal.
5 A baleen whale is a modern marine mammal.

6 Today, chemicals and other toxic wastes, like this oil can, are dumped into oceans.
7 A blue-ringed octopus is a modern animal from Australia.
8 Today fishing nets, like this drift net left floating in the ocean, kill many water animals.

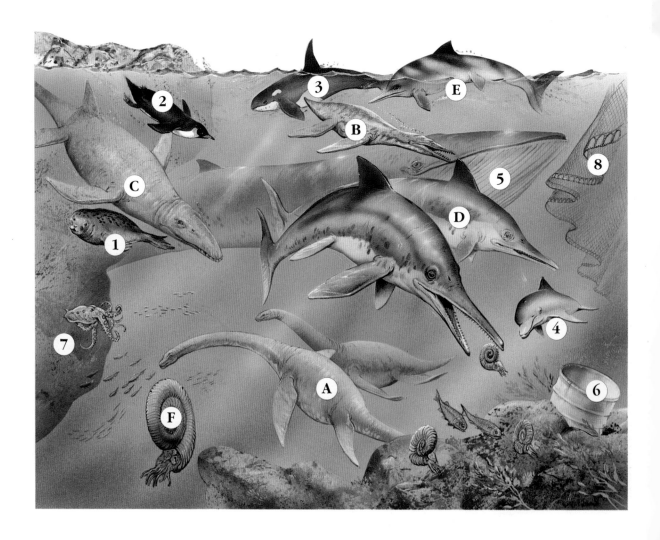

Muraenosaurus (A) was a stout, rigid-bodied plesiosaur with a very long snakelike neck. The head was tiny. Plesiosaurs probably fed on fish and squidlike animals. Their long necks helped them raise their heads high above the water to search for signs of their prey.

Peloneustes (B) was a short-necked pliosaur. Pliosaurs were fierce, streamlined hunters.

Fact file

Ammonites were the most abundant soft-bodied animals that lived in oceans. They were related to today's octopus and squid. Like the pearly nautilus that lives in warm oceans today, their body was protected by a coiled shell. A variety of ammonites developed. Each species had a different shaped shell. Some lived on the ocean floor, but most were probably fast swimmers.

Like modern squid, ammonites probably swam by jet propulsion. They sucked water in and then squeezed it out to push themselves along. Like the dinosaurs, most ammonites died out at the end of the Cretaceous Period.

Titanites

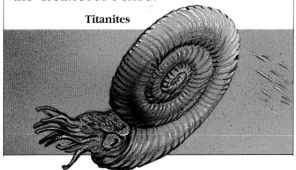

They probably preyed on sharks, squid, ichthyosaurs, and even their relatives, the plesiosaurs. They may have used their flippers to swim fast like today's seals and sea lions. Peloneustes probably ate squidlike animals and ammonites. Its long head helped it reach out to catch its prey.

Liopleurodon (C) was a large pliosaur. This whalelike predator grew up to 39 feet (12 m) long. Like modern whales, Liopleurodon had a streamlined body, with a large head and hardly any visible neck. It may have hunted ammonites.

Ichthyosaurs, like Ichthyosaurus (D) and Stenopterygius (E), were reptiles that were well suited to life in the ocean. Their bodies were shaped like fast-swimming fish. They gave birth to live young instead of laying eggs. This means that they never left the ocean. Like modern dolphins, ichthyosaurs probably sped after their prey. They may also have leaped above the waves.

Titanites (F) was a large marine ammonite. It looked very like the nautilus of today. These distant relatives of octopus and squid had beautiful coiled shells.

Dinosaur Differences...

Dinosaurs are some of the most famous prehistoric reptiles. Tyrannosaurus rex was probably one of the most frightening. Look carefully at these pictures of its home in North America, 75 million years ago. Can you spot the ten differences between them?

Dinosaurs were a group of reptiles that lived for 200 million years. They developed into many **species** that spread across the world. Like most reptiles, dinosaurs laid eggs. Fossil nests have been found with eggs and young dinosaur "chicks." Most reptiles were cold-blooded animals. No one is sure if dinosaurs were cold-blooded or warm-blooded.

Tyrannosaurus was the largest land predator known. It had strong hind legs and could have ran after its prey. Tyrannosaurus may have attacked with its mouth wide open. It used its sharp, dagger-like teeth to tear at its prey. Some scientists think Tyrannosaurus may not have been an active hunter. They think it may have fed on dead animals.

On Display

Did you spot all ten differences?

1 Euoplocephalus's head plates are different.
2 Tyrannosaurus rex has one claw missing.
3 A Stegoceras has lost its head crest.
4 Triceratops's nose horn is missing.
5 An Anatosaurus has food in its mouth.
6 Velociraptor has joined Dromaeosaurus.

7 An Apatosaurus's head has changed position. Diplodocus is grazing with them.
8 A Corythosaurus now looks like another dinosaur called Parasaurolophus.
9 A lizard is now near the small mammal.
10 Troodon has caught the shrewlike mammal.

Not all predators were big. Troodon was only 6 feet (2 m) long. It had large eyes and may have hunted small mammals and lizards at night. Troodon may have hunted in packs like modern wolves.

Velociraptor and Dromaeosaurus were similar dinosaurs to Troodon. They were active hunters with sharp, pointed teeth and clawed front feet. All three dinosaurs had a large, sharp curved claw on each hind foot. They probably used it to slash their prey.

With such dangerous predators around, plant-eating dinosaurs had to protect themselves. The skin of Euoplocephalus was covered with bony plates to form a flexible shield. This 18-feet (5.5-m) long dinosaur had a stiff tail with a bony club on the end. When the animal swung around quickly, the club may have acted as a weapon. It could have caused great damage.

Triceratops was a large dinosaur with three horns. A wide bony shield grew from the back of its head. This could have protected it against predators biting it from above.

Herds of duck-billed dinosaurs, such as Anatosaurus, probably roamed the land like grazing buffalo.

Some, such as Corythosaurus, had head crests. Parasaurolophus had a hollow tube on its head that may have made a sound like a trombone. These animals may have hooted to each other. Stegoceras, especially the males, had a thick top to the skull. Perhaps males head-butted each other like deer and goats do today.

Apatosaurus and Diplodocus were among the largest plant-eating dinosaurs. Both dinosaurs probably reared up on their hind legs when grazing on tall trees. They may have used the tail like a third leg for balance. Their long necks could then reach the treetops. They were the giraffes of the dinosaur world.

Fact file

Diplodocus was one of the longest dinosaurs. It reached 85 feet (26 m) from nose to tail.

Tyrannosaurus was 20 feet (6 m) tall. From nose to tail it measured 49 feet (15 m).

Rulers of the Skies

While dinosaurs ruled the land, the pterosaurs were masters of the air. These amazing reptiles probably flew in much the same way as today's birds. Look at this picture of a seashore during Cretaceous times, about 140 million years ago. Can you spot the eight animals that would not have lived then?

The first pterosaurs lived long before modern birds developed. Pterosaurs first appeared about 230 million years ago. Like bats, pterosaurs had long, narrow wings made of skin. The skin was stretched along the arm bones and the bones of one very long finger. Pterosaurs could probably flap their wings and fly like a bird. Like birds, pterosaurs may also have been warm-blooded. A few pterosaurs have been found with their bodies covered in fine fur.

Some pterosaurs were the size of a small bird. Others were much bigger! Quetzalcoatlus (A) had a wingspan of up to 40 feet (12 m). It was the largest flying animal known. Quetzalcoatlus flew inland and may have eaten dead animals, like vultures do today.

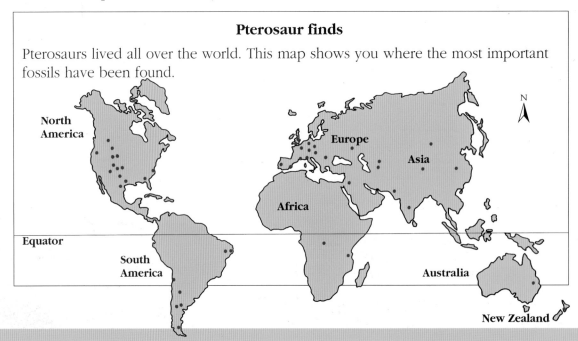

Pterosaur finds

Pterosaurs lived all over the world. This map shows you where the most important fossils have been found.

North America

Europe

Asia

Africa

Equator

South America

Australia

New Zealand

N

Flying High

Pterosaurs probably laid eggs like most reptiles. They may have built nests like today's seabirds. Perhaps they nested on cliffs and beaches, or on the top of trees. Most fossil pterosaurs are found in rocks that were laid down in seawater. This suggests that they lived like modern seabirds. Other pterosaurs may have lived inland, but their fossils were not as easily preserved.

On land, scientists think that pterosaurs may have crawled on all fours like bats. Some pterosaurs may have walked on their hind legs, folding their wings like a bird's.

Pterosaurs lived right across the world and may have had lifestyles similar to those of modern birds. Ornithocheirus (B) lived by the Cretaceous seashore. Like today's gulls, it may have caught fish in its narrow, toothed jaws.

Cearadactylus (C) had special front teeth that fitted closely together. It probably fished in shallow water. Tropeognathus (D) had large rounded crests on the end of its jaws. Perhaps it plucked fish from the water. These crests may have kept the animal's head from swinging from side to side as it fished.

Small Batrachognathus (E) may have caught flying insects. It had a short head and wide mouth like today's nightjar or swift. These birds feed on flying insects.

First birds

Archaeopteryx is the earliest known bird. It lived during the Late Jurassic Period, about 175 million years ago. It was the size of a modern pigeon with a small head and large eyes. It ate insects and glided from tree to tree. Unlike modern birds, Archaeopteryx had a long bony tail. It also had sharp pointed teeth in its jaws and claws on its wings. Its skeleton was very much like that of a dinosaur group called the coelurosaurs. It was like modern birds in two ways. It had a wishbone and feathers. Most modern groups of birds did not appear until 55-100 million years ago.

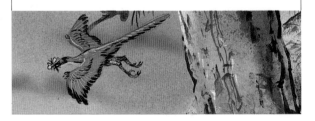

Pterodaustro (F) had rows of long bristles on its jaws. Like a flamingo, it may have filtered food from shallow water. A set of short, blunt teeth in its upper jaw chopped the food up into small pieces.

Huge Pteranodon (G) probably ate fish. It had a wingspan of up to 30 feet (9 m). It may have soared over the ocean's surface like an albatross. Different Pteranodon species had different shaped crests.

Dsungaripterus (H) had long pointed jaws like a pair of tweezers. Like modern wading birds, it could have used its jaws to probe for food. Dsungaripterus may have fed on snails, worms, shellfish, and other such animals. Blunt, bony knobs at the back of its jaws could have been used to crack open the shellfish.

Some dinosaurs may also have eaten fish. Baryonyx (I) had jaws like a crocodile. It also had a large, curved claw, probably on its front feet. Some scientists think it ate fish. Maybe it hooked fish out of the water like brown bears do today.

Eight odd ones out

These modern animals all eat fish or other foods that may have been eaten by pterosaurs.

1   A brown bear fishing.
2   A nightjar catching insects.
3   A vulture searching for dead animals.
4   Flamingos feeding.
5   A sea otter eating shellfish.
6   A tern diving for fish.
7   A fishing bat.
8   The platypus from Australia lives on shellfish and small water creatures.

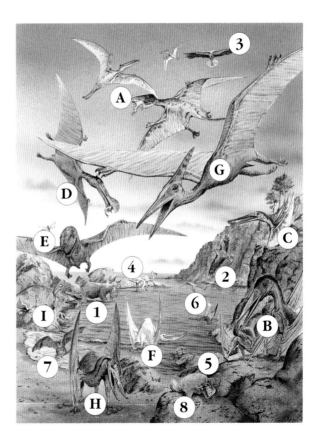

A New Age

The dinosaurs died out at the end of the Cretaceous Period. They were replaced by the mammals. Look at this picture of a clearing in an Eocene forest, 50 million years ago. Can you help the lemurlike Notharctus (A) find the one open, safe path to rejoin its family (B)?

Who are the primitive primates?

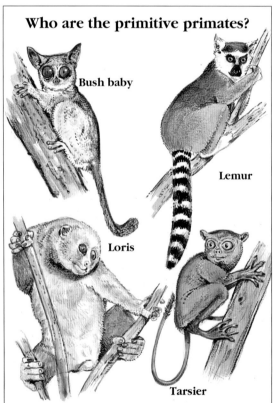

Bush baby

Lemur

Loris

Tarsier

The primates are a group of mammals that developed from an insect-eating tree shrew. Here are some primitive primates that are still alive today.

Monkeys, apes, and man are all advanced primates.

At the end of the Cretaceous Period, the remaining dinosaur species died out. Some scientists believe that a major disaster happened. Maybe a meteorite hit Earth. Others think that the climate changed. The dinosaurs could not adapt to the changed habitats and so they died out.

While the dinosaurs had ruled, small insect-eating mammals had lived by their side. They survived by lurking in the undergrowth and only coming out at night. After the dinosaurs died out, these mammals were able to fill these new daytime habitats.

By the Eocene Period, mammals had spread across the world. They now appeared as many different species. Some were the ancestors of animals we know today.

Mighty Mammals

Notharctus was an early lemurlike primate. Primates are the group of animals that include lemurs, apes, monkeys, and humans. Notharctus was a tree-dwelling animal. It had good vision. Also, its hands and feet could hold onto branches and food.

Notharctus had many predators in its forest home. Hyaenodon was a large dog-like predator. It was related to Oxyaena, a heavy animal that looked like today's wolverine. Both were creodonts, an early type of carnivore. They were hunters and **scavengers**. The creodonts were eventually replaced by other carnivores that were faster and more intelligent.

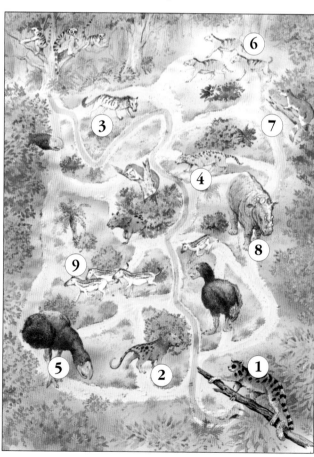

Did you beat the maze?

Did you help Notharctus find the only open, safe path home?

1   Notharctus

Dangerous predators ready to attack:

2   Hyaenodon
3   Oxyaena
4   Mesonyx
5   Diatryma

Harmless plant eaters blocking the way:

6   Phenacodus
7   Paramys
8   Uintatherium
9   Hyracotherium

Mighty carnivores

Creodonts like Hyaenodon and Oxyaena were the main meat-eaters in the Eocene Period. Some were the size of a weasel. Others were as large as a grizzly bear. They were fierce hunters and scavengers. By the Late Miocene, some 7 million years ago, they had all died out. Their place had been taken by the true carnivores. This group, called the Carnivora, includes modern cats, dogs, bears, and seals. Many early carnivores, like Smilodon, had huge biting canine teeth. Their teeth were much larger than those of the big cats today.

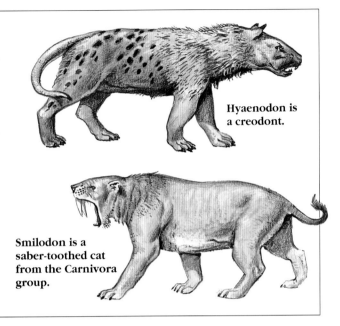

Hyaenodon is a creodont.

Smilodon is a saber-toothed cat from the Carnivora group.

Mesonyx was another large hyenalike animal. Surprisingly it was related to plant-eating animals such as Phenacodus. Mesonyx had five-toed feet but with small hooves rather than claws.

Rodents are a group of mammals that includes rats, mice, beavers, and squirrels. They first appeared about 60 million years ago. Paramys was an early squirrel-like rodent.

In its day, Uintatherium was the largest mammal. About the size of a rhinoceros, these plant-eating animals had six horns. They also had very large tusks.

Hyracotherium is sometimes called the "dawn horse." It was like the ancestor of modern horses. Today's horses have only one toe, or hoof. Hyracotherium had four toes on the front feet and three toes on the back. But it used one toe more than the rest.

When the dinosaurs died out, there were probably no very large predators left in the world. Several large birds developed to fill the gap. Diatryma was one. This giant, flightless predator grew to 7 feet (2 m) tall. It had a huge head with a beak like an eagle's. Many scientists believe that Diatryma was one of the fiercest and most dangerous predators that lived in Eocene times.

8

Who's Who?

During the Oligocene, different kinds of mammals developed. Some of them were ancestors of today's animal groups. Look at this scene of an Oligocene open woodland. Can you match up the animals with the modern relatives shown in the small pictures?

The Oligocene Period was about 35 million years ago. Then, much of North America and Europe was covered by open woodland and scrublike grasslands. It was home to many different mammals. Some of these were distant relatives, or early forms, of animals alive today.

Paracricetodon, a small rodentlike mammal, was like the ancestor of modern rats, mice, lemmings, and voles. Trigonias was an early type of rhinoceros, a group of animals that once had more species than they do today. Trigonias did not have horns. Unlike modern rhinos, which have three toes, Trigonius had five toes.

Modern Relatives

Did you match them up?

1 Peltephilus was an early armadillo.
2 Poebrotherium was an early camel.
3 Palaeolagus was an early rabbit.
4 Phiomia was an early elephant.
5 Paracricetodon was an early rodent.

6 Trigonius was an early rhinoceros.
7 Hesperocyon was an early dog.
8 Dinictis belonged to the cat family.
9 Mesohippus was an early horse.
10 Entelodon was an early boar.

Another early kind of rhino, Indricotherium, was the largest known land mammal. Its shoulders were 18 feet (5 m) high, and it was 26 feet (8 m) long.

Mesohippus was an early horse, about as big as a large dog. It had three toes on its feet. The middle toe was larger than the rest.

Peltephilus, a type of armadillo, may have eaten meat. Its back was covered with bony plates. This armadillo looked unusual, with two horns on its nose.

Phiomia, an elephant, lived at the edges of the woods. It had short tusks and a short trunk. Its lower front teeth were long and shaped like a huge scoop. They were probably used for gathering food. Poebrotherium, an early camel, also lived in open woods. It had only two toes on its feet and could probably run quite quickly.

Many hunters lived here, too. Hesperocyon, a small dog, may have hunted in packs. Perhaps Dinictis, an early cat, lived like today's leopards and African wildcats.

Other smaller mammals lived on grasslands. Palaeolagus, one of the first rabbits, ran rather than hopped.

How did horses develop?

Horses evolved as they changed their lifestyle. The first horses were small browsers that grazed on leaves in forests. Their descendants became large, swiftly running animals grazing in open grasslands. Some early horses like Parahippus moved from the forest into the grasslands. There was more room to move and large areas of grassland to graze. As they became adapted to their new habitat, the horses' feet slowly changed. The outer toes were lost and hard hooves developed. Modern horses only have one large central toe and a hoof on each foot.

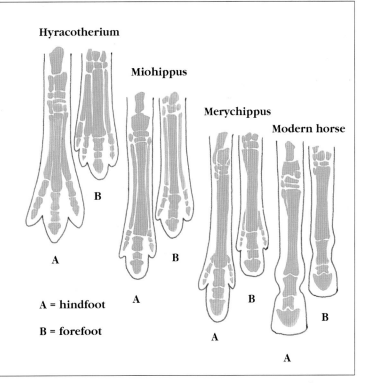

Hyracotherium
Miohippus
Merychippus
Modern horse

A = hindfoot
B = forefoot

9

The Age of Mammals

During the Miocene Period, 15 million years ago, vast herds of grazing mammals lived on wide, open grasslands. Look carefully at these two pictures. See if you can spot the ten differences between them.

The climate in the Miocene became cooler. Fewer trees grew and grasses began to grow over wide areas of land. Vast grassy plains and prairies developed.

The animals that lived here included herds of grazing animals. Parahippus was an early horse. Herds of these animals galloped across these plains. Synthetoceras, a strange deerlike animal, had three horns. Two straight horns grew between the ears. Males also had a Y-shaped horn on the end of their noses!

Stenomylus was a small animal related to camels. It looked like a deer and may have lived in herds.

Across the Plains

Aepycamelus was a very tall camel. It was 10 feet (3 m) high at the head. It could easily have browsed on tall plants.

Moropus looked like a huge horse. It had large feet armed with massive claws. Moropus may have eaten plants or dug up roots with its claws. Dinohyus was a giant piglike animal with a long muzzle. It grew to the size of a bull. Dinohyus probably sniffed in the grass eating anything it could find. No relatives of these two animals are alive today.

Gomphotherium was a common elephant during the Miocene. It had four straight tusks, two in its upper jaw and two in its lower jaw. Some species lived on the plains, others lived in swamps. They all ate plants.

Predators such as the doglike Daphaenodon probably hunted in packs. Like cheetahs, they could run quickly across the open plains.

Grass grazers

Grass is a much tougher plant food than leaves. As a result, animals that graze on grass developed special teeth and stomachs. Their front teeth are specially shaped to help them cut the grass. Their back teeth then grind the grass into tiny pieces. Animals like cows, horses, deer, sheep, and camels "chew the cud." The grass is eaten, chewed, and swallowed. Later the swallowed grass, called cud, is brought back up into the mouth. It is then chewed again. This helps the animals get as much nourishment from the grass as possible. The teeth of Miocene camels, deer, and horses show that these animals probably chewed the cud, too.

Synthetoceras

Deinogalerix, a giant hedgehog, probably ate insects and worms. Or it may have been a scavenger.

Birds like Osteodontornis flew in the skies. Few fossils have survived because bird bones are so fragile.

Did you spot the ten differences?

1 Moropus has a root in its claw.

2 A Parahippus is missing.

3 Aepycamelus has food in its mouth.

4 Synthetoceras's nose horn is different.

5 Another Stenomylus is sitting down.

6 Dinohyus's tail can be seen.

7 A Gomphotherium's tusks are missing.

8 A Daphaenodon's ears are down.

9 Deinogalerix is about to eat a beetle.

10 One Osteodontornis is a different color.

Food for Thought

The animals in this picture all eat different foods. Can you guess who eats what? Match the animals with their food shown in the six small pictures.

The remains of dinosaurs and prehistoric animals are a mass of fossilized bones and teeth. From these, scientists have to rebuild the animal. They try to find out how the animal lived. The shape of different teeth can tell us the type of food the animals ate. Several fossils may be found together. Did they die as hunter and prey? Or did they have nothing to do with each other?

Direct evidence of an animal's food is rarely found. In a few fossils the contents of the stomach have been fossilized. Some bones found with teeth and claw marks can be matched to a predator. In the end scientists have to be detectives and guess what may have happened.

Dinnertime

What's for dinner?

1 Diplodocus ate conifer leaves.

2 Stegosaurus ate leaves from small trees and other plants like cycads.

3 Archaeopteryx probably glided from tree to tree and ate insects.

4 Pterodactylus probably caught fish and may have probed for worms.

5 Ornitholestes probably caught lizards and small mammals.

6 Allosaurus hunted Camptosaurus, which ate small ground plants.

In this Jurassic scene a pack of Allosaurus are hunting a herd of Camptosaurus. Camptosaurus ate plants. It probably pulled off leaves and small twigs with its toothless beak. Allosaurus also hunted other plant eaters such as Dryosaurus (A). These small deerlike dinosaurs probably grazed on ground plants.

Diplodocus was the longest dinosaur. Scientists now think that they stripped pine needles from conifer trees. They could even stand up on their hind legs to reach the highest branches. Their long tails may have been used as a prop to keep them from falling over.

Stegosaurus may have eaten plants such as cycads and ferns. It probably stood up on its hind legs to feed from the tops of small trees.

Ornitholestes was a fairly small frisky predator. It probably hunted small lizards and mammals. It could have reached out grasped them in its powerful clawed hands. It had a strong jaw and sharp teeth for ripping flesh.

High above, pterosaurs flew across the sky. Many may have swooped down to catch fish from lagoons and seas. Pterodactylus probably ate fish. It may also have probed the soft sand with its narrow beak looking for worms.

Archaeopteryx, one of the earliest known birds, also lived in Jurassic times. It was about the size of a modern pigeon. Archaeopteryx lived in trees, probably feeding on the insects it found there. Unlike modern birds, Archaeopteryx had small sharp teeth in its jaws.

What are gizzard stones?

Like chickens eating grit, Stegosaurus and many other large plant-eating dinosaurs often ate stones. Large stones stayed in the gizzard part of their stomach and helped to grind up the huge quantities of tough plant food that these animals ate.

The stones eventually became quite rounded and polished. They are called gizzard stones.

Glossary

Adapted Changed over long periods of time. An animal or plant becomes adapted to fit in its habitat to help it survive more easily.

Ancestor The animals or plants from which particular individuals have descended. For example, your great, great grandparents are your ancestors.

Cartilage A gristly, flexible material that forms the skeleton in some animals. (See skeleton.)

Cold-blooded Describes an animal whose body temperature changes with the temperature of its surroundings. In cold weather the animal's body temperature falls. In hot weather, its temperature rises.

Descendants An animal or plant that has descended through generations from a relative of the past. For example, you are the descendant of your great, great grandparents.

Fossils The remains of plants or animals that died a long time ago and which became buried in rock and turned to stone.

Habitat The place in which an animal or plant lives. Habitats include deserts, rain forests, grassland, mountains, and seashores. Each type of animal or plant fits best in one or a few habitats.

Larva (plural **larvae**) The young of certain animals, such as some insects and frogs. The larva hatches from the egg and often looks quite different from its parents.

Marine Describes an animal or plant that lives in saltwater habitats such as oceans.

Predator An animal that kills and eats other animals.

Prey An animal that is killed and eaten by another animal.

Scavenger An animal that eats dead animals and plants.

Skeleton The hard parts that form the framework of an animal's body. It gives shape to the body. It protects and supports the soft parts inside the body.

Species A group of animals or plants that all look similar. They can mate with each other to produce young.

Streamlined Describes a shape that is pointed or rounded at the front and narrows gradually toward the end. Such shapes move faster in air and water.

Warm-blooded Describes an animal whose body temperature stays the same whatever the temperature of its surroundings. Birds and mammals are warm-blooded.

Index

A Templar Book

Devised and produced by The Templar Company plc
Pippbrook Mill, London Road, Dorking, Surrey RH4 1JE, Great Britain
© Copyright 1996 by The Templar Company plc